Putting Your Angels To Work

Putting Your Angels To Work

by
Norvel Hayes

HARRISON HOUSE
Tulsa, Oklahoma

Unless otherwise indicated, all Scripture quotations
are taken from the *King James Version* of the Bible.

Putting Your Angels To Work
(Formerly *What Makes Angels Work*)
ISBN 0-89274-571-1
Copyright © 1989 by Norvel Hayes
P. O. Box 1379
Cleveland, Tennessee 37311

Published by Harrison House, Inc.
P.O. Box 35035
Tulsa, Oklahoma 74153

Contents

Introduction

Several years ago Charles Capps, a great teacher of God's Word, came to our Bible school in Cleveland, Tennessee, where he taught on angels. That man sure can teach on angels! During that meeting the Lord dealt with me real strong about this subject. He unfolded to me from the Scriptures the truth about angels and their ministry. It is this truth which I want to share with you in this book.

Today as never before, we Christians need to know about angels. We need to know that angels do minister to us and for us. Hebrews 1:14 says about angels, **Are they not all ministering spirits, sent forth to minister for them who shall be heirs of salvation?** Angels minister in many different ways, but they always minister on orders from God. They are holy creatures sent by God to carry out His will.

But angels can disobey their Lord just as we humans can. Remember that Satan and his demons are disobedient angels. They used to serve God in heaven, but then they rebelled against Him and were cast out of His presence. That's why we have this great spiritual warfare going on right now between the spiritual forces of good and the rebellious forces of evil.

We human beings have the power of choice. We can decide whether we want to obey God or not. But an angel *must* obey God or else be cast out of His presence. When an angel is obedient, he must not only do *what* God commands, he must also do it *as* God commands. Angels always work in line with the Holy Spirit and the Bible. That is a lesson we believers should take note of and learn for ourselves.

Since angels are ministering spirits sent to minister to and for us Christians, in this book we will see how to activate our angels, how to put them into action on our behalf.

Learn To Please God

What do I mean when I talk about "putting your angels to work"? I mean that since angels are spirits sent by God to carry out His will on this earth by ministering to and for the "heirs of salvation," then we believers ought to be keeping those angelic creatures busy! We ought to have them working for us all the time.

"But how do we do that?" you may ask. "How do I put my angels to work?"

The answer is simple: by pleasing God. Since angels take instruction from God and work according to what the Bible says, as long as you are *speaking* and *acting* in a way that pleases God and conforms to His Word, then angels will minister to you and for you.

But the opposite is also true. If you don't speak and act in a way pleasing to God and according to what His Word says, then His holy angels will not minister to you or for you. They will stand off at a distance and watch you, but they won't minister.

If you want your angels to go to work to help you, then you've got to do the things that please God! You've got to please *God!*

"But how?" you ask.

There are seven basic ways a Christian pleases God. We will look at them one by one.

1
Have Faith

But without faith it is impossible to please him: for he that cometh to God must believe that he is, and that he is a rewarder of them that diligently seek him.

Hebrews 11:6

How do you please God? The first thing you must do to please God is to have faith. For your angels to work, faith must be in operation. Angels will not minister to you or for you unless you have faith in God, faith that lines up with His Word.

The more you believe God — the more your words and actions conform to His Word — the more He can and will do for you. So if you will just sell out to God, believing everything you read in the Bible, then you will be on your way to a life filled with joy and victory, because the angels of the Lord will encamp around about you. They will always be there to work on your behalf.

Some people are afraid to sell out totally to God. That is a mistake. The smartest thing I ever did in my life was to get on my knees and put my life entirely into the hands of the Lord. That was the day I really began to live.

The greatest prayer I ever prayed was the one when I asked the Lord to take charge of my life, to teach me how to live and love His way. I had come to the place in my life where I wanted all that God had for me. But I knew that in order to get all God had *for* me, I had to give Him all *of* me.

Faith Leads to Commitment

That's where faith comes in: you cannot hold onto a part of your life and still expect to receive God's best. You have to let go of everything you have, then God can give you everything He has. To really receive from God, you have to trust Him. And in order to trust Him, you have to believe Him. That's what faith is, believing God: **For what saith the scripture? Abraham believed God, and it was counted unto him for righteousness** (Rom. 4:3). It pleases God when we *believe* Him. (Heb. 11:6.)

That's what I did that day I turned my life over to the Lord. I just decided that come what may I was going to believe God. I wasn't going to mind what anyone thought or said or did; I was going to find out what God said and believe it and do it. I told the Lord that I was going to believe all of the Bible. No matter what it said, I was going to believe it. I was going to forget about my denominational title. I wasn't going to worry about what my family or friends or church thought. I was going to read and believe the Bible, putting it into action in my life. Whatever it said, that's what I was going to do. I was going to be a doer of the Word and not just a hearer only! (James 1:22.)

Faith Leads to Action

I decided that I was going to follow the Holy Ghost and not men. When I began to read the Word, the first thing I discovered was that Jesus said, **Verily, verily, I say unto you, He that believeth on me, the works that I do shall he do also; and greater works than these shall he do; because I go unto my Father** (John 14:12). So the first thing I saw was that faith leads to action.

Then I read Mark 16:17,18 and I saw what action I was to take: **And these signs shall follow them that believe; In my name shall they cast out devils; they shall speak with**

new tongues;...they shall lay hands on the sick, and they shall recover.

So I said to myself, "If Jesus said that those who believe in Him will cast out devils, then that's what I'm going to do."

Immediately Satan whispered in my ear, "But if you do that, your friends will think you're crazy."

"That's all right," I answered, "who cares what they think!"

"Yes, but what about your family?" the devil asked. "What about your relatives? They all belong to a church that doesn't believe in casting out devils. What will they say about you?"

"I don't know, and what's more I don't care!" I declared. And that was the end of that conversation.

You see, that's the place you have to come to if you really want to please God. You have to care more about what God thinks than you do about what people think. You have to decide that you want to please your heavenly Father more than you want to win the approval of other people.

That doesn't mean that you have to defy your family and friends or turn your back on them. It just means that you don't allow your life to be determined by someone else's convictions. You take responsibility for your own decisions. In love you explain to your loved ones what you are doing and why you believe God wants you to do it. But then whether they agree or not, you listen to the voice of God rather than the voice of men. That's faith.

Faith Leads to Obedience

In the third chapter of Matthew's Gospel, we find the story of Jesus' baptism. You remember how Jesus came to John the Baptist and asked to be baptized of him. But John was so humble he wanted to get out of the Lord's will by having Jesus baptize him. He said, "No, Lord, this isn't right. I ought to be baptized of *you!*" But what did Jesus tell him? **Suffer it to be so now: for thus it becometh us to fulfil all righteousness** (Matt. 3:15). In other words He was saying, "John, if we are to please God, we must listen to His Spirit and do this thing God's way." Jesus said John was the greatest man who ever lived (Matt. 11:11) — besides Himself. One reason John the Baptist was so great was because he believed the Lord and did what He said to do. Because he had faith in God, he was obedient to Him. Because of his belief and obedience, God put His Spirit into John. We have that same Holy Spirit in us.

Jesus Himself said of the Father, **And he that sent me is with me: the Father hath not left me alone; for I do always those things that please him** (John 8:29). And what did the Father say when Jesus came up out of those baptismal waters? **This is my beloved Son, in whom I am well pleased** (Matt. 3:17).

It pleases God when His children believe Him. It also pleases Him when they are obedient, when they do what He says to do. This kind of thinking, believing, acting and obeying will cause the angels of God to come and minister to us and for us.

Faith Leads to Ministry

So then we accept the Bible by faith. Without faith, it is impossible to please God. *If we don't please God, the angels will not come and exercise their ministry to us.*

The ministry of the angels to us is much greater than most people ever think about. Oh, sure, they are sent to protect us and keep us from dashing our foot against a stone. (Matt. 4:6.) But that is only the beginning. In reality, their ministry goes far beyond just keeping us from getting a broken toe!

Angels can minister almost anything to us. They are ministering spirits sent from heaven to help us in our time of need. Most people never realize that angels are in the ministry of helps. (1 Cor. 12:28.)

Most Christians don't really care much for the ministry of helps. It sounds too much like work and self-sacrifice. Many Christians tell me, "Oh, Brother Norvel, the ministry of helps is not for me; that's just not my calling."

"Sure it is," I tell them, "How could it not be? God makes it very plain in His Word that if you have two coats, you are to give one to somebody who doesn't have one. And that doesn't just apply to coats, it also means food, money, prayer — even time. As Christians, we are *all* in the ministry of helps. That's what we're on his earth for, to bring glory to God by helping other people. If you're a believer, then you *are* in the ministry of helps — like it or not!"

If you are born again by the Spirit of God, then you are under orders to be in the ministry of helps for as long as you live on this earth. This means helping others whenever they need help. It means living your life to be a blessing to others.

To receive God's blessings, we must do what He says to do. If we expect to be ministered to by God's angels, then we have to be ready to minister to others. *Angels minister to us; we minister to others!* That's God's will and plan.

If you want to be blessed, be a blessing. If you want to be ministered to, minister to someone else. If you want the angels to serve you, be pleasing to God. And the Number One way to please God is to have faith.

2

Get To Know the Lord

God is a Spirit: and they that worship him must worship
him in spirit and in truth.

John 4:24

In order to please God, a person has to know the Lord
personally. Jesus Christ is a personal Savior. He wants a
personal relationship with each one of us.

God is a Spirit. He lives on the inside of each believer.
God, the Holy Spirit, who inhabits your earthly body does
not think any differently from God the Father who lives in
heaven. Father, Son and Holy Ghost all think and speak in
line with God's Word. Whatever the Word of God says, that's
the way it is. You might as well make up your mind to accept
that truth and to learn to live by it!

Jesus said that those who worship God must worship
Him **in spirit and in truth.** That is, in word and deed. That
means that you must come to the place that you will humble
yourself before God and worship and praise Him with your
own mouth. God wants to hear words from your mouth —
words of worship and praise to Him personally — all day
long. Then He wants you to complete your worship by going
forth into the world to live for Him day by day. The Apostle
Paul talks about presenting our *bodies* a living sacrifice, holy,
acceptable unto God, which is our reasonable service. (Rom.
12:1.)

If you will do that, if you will continually worship and
praise the Lord in spirit and in truth (spiritually and
physically), then He will see to it that all your needs are met.

He has promised to do so: **But seek ye first the kingdom of God, and his righteousness; and all these things** (you need) **shall be added unto you** (Matt. 6:33).

I haven't had any unfulfilled needs in years. Not weeks or months. *Years.* I haven't had a sad day in my life for ages. I don't ever intend to have another one. As long as I live, I never intend to have a sad day or a confused day. In fact, I don't put up with confused days. If the devil comes in and tries to cause confusion in my life, I do just what I would do if someone came into my place of business to cause a disturbance: I tell him to get out! I say, "Satan, in the name of Jesus, you get out of here right now!" And he gets! The air clears up and everything is back to normal in no time flat. You see, you can't keep demons from showing up for work, but you can sure see that they don't make any time off you!

Jesus paid the price for you to live the abundant life. He did not suffer untold agony and pain so you could live a sick, beaten down, confused, wondering life. He has made plenty of provision for victory and peace and abundance in every area of your life. You just need to learn to appropriate what is rightfully yours. You do that by worshipping, praising and serving the Lord your God.

If you will get to know the Lord, you will begin to understand what all He has done for you in Jesus Christ. You will come to realize and know who you are in Christ. You will start to think and act like a child of the King instead of like a beggar in the streets. You will begin to learn to exercise the authority and power that is yours as an heir of God and joint-heir with Jesus. Then as you worship your Lord, as you allow Him to fill you with His strong, sweet Spirit, you will begin to walk in the abundance and peace and victory that is yours. As you seek first God and His righteousness, then you will see all the good things of life that you need come flowing in to you.

The prophet Daniel tells us, **...the people that do know their God shall be strong, and do exploits** (Dan. 11:32). Since you now know Him, what "exploits" are you supposed to do? We know that we are all called into the ministry of helps. But what is your *specific* calling in the Kingdom of God?

3

Find Your Calling

The most important thing you will ever do in this life is to find your calling. *Find God's plan for you and walk in it.*

As you do, the angels will minister to you, for you, and through you.

God Has Something for You To Do

Remember that John the Baptist operated by the Spirit of God which dwelled in him, and that same Spirit dwells in us today. But although we have the same Spirit in us that John had, none of us will manifest the same personality as John. God gives each of us talents by the Holy Spirit to bring forth the ministry that fits us well and that He's called us to do.

God gave John the Baptist a rugged spirit. That's the reason he preached as he did. Now you and I can't expect to go out and preach like John the Baptist. We're not supposed to. Not everyone has been called to the same type of ministry. You need to discover what the Lord has in mind for you individually. Then you need to develop the spirit which the Lord has placed within you for the specific ministry He wants you to fulfill.

If you will do that, God will train and condition your spirit. The more you do for Him, the more you will come into His perfect will for you. The more you do that, the more talents will come forth from your spirit. When you sell out totally to God, then He will begin to manifest Himself *to* you and *through* you. If you don't sell out completely, you will only receive a part of what God has for you.

Man's Way Vs. God's Way

John the Baptist was a man who was sold out to God. Completely. Any man who lives out in the wild, living off locusts and honey as John did, has to be sold out. Otherwise he wouldn't have done it. But even John became confused when Jesus came to him to be baptized of him.

When John told Jesus that He had things backwards, that he was the one who needed to be baptized of Him, that statement was out of the will of God. That was not what John the Baptist had been chosen and trained to do. God had already told him that he was the one who was to baptize the Messiah. John knew who Jesus was the minute he laid eyes on Him. But when John looked up and saw standing before him Jesus, **the Lamb of God, which taketh away the sin of the world** (John 1:29), because of a false sense of humility he almost missed his divine appointment. He tried to change God's script. He wanted Jesus to baptize him, instead of fulfilling the plan and ministry God had ordained for him from the foundation of the earth.

You see, we cannot tell God how to do things. It's stupid of us to even think of such a thing. It's ridiculous for a group of men to get together and build a church, put a steeple on top of it, hire a preacher, and then try to tell God how to run His church. It won't work! And it is not pleasing to God.

John had to please God by fulfiling the Word. So do you and I. We please God by fulfilling the plan and purpose He has for us as individuals and as a church.

A Lesson From Kenneth Hagin

Let me give you an example of fulfilling God's plan. After Brother Kenneth Hagin had worked in the ministry for fourteen years, one night the Lord spoke to him and said, "Son, now I'm going to place you in the first phase of your ministry."

Brother Hagin was so shocked he almost couldn't talk. "Dear God," he choked, "You mean I've been working for You for fourteen years and I've not yet even entered the *first* phase of my ministry?"

"That's right," answered the Lord.

"But I've served as a pastor for fourteen years."

"Yes, I know," the Lord responded. "But I never called you to be a pastor."

"You didn't?"

"No, you became a pastor because when I called you to preach and teach, you thought that was the only way to fulfill that call. Since the door was open to become a pastor, that's what you did. But it wasn't My doing. I never called you to serve as a pastor."

"You didn't?"

"No, but since you were sincere and stayed in the Word, I honored your commitment and decision. Because you let My Holy Spirit work through you, I was able to accomplish a great deal of good. I helped you all I could, but the decision to enter the pastorate was yours, not Mine. You worked for Me for fourteen years all right, but you were never in My perfect will. I called you to teach My Word."

So Brother Hagin worked for God for fourteen long years before the Lord ever promoted him to the ministry of prophet and teacher. It's good that God honored his commitment all those years and finally led him into his true ministry, but that's not God's best. The best way is to find God's will from the beginning and walk in it.

Find Your Place

Remember that *all* Christians are called to the ministry of the Word in some form or another. You will never really please God until you find your place in His overall plan of ministry. You will never really be pleasing to God unless you are helping Jesus spread the Gospel.

Now you might think that being a nice, clean, upstanding citizen with two cars and a nice home and a fat bank account is enough to make you happy. But it isn't. Not if you are a child of God. Neither home nor family nor wealth nor pleasure nor fame nor any other thing in this world — as good as it may be — will ever satisfy that inner hunger you will experience. When you were born again, you were reborn with a mission. Until you find and fulfill that mission, you will never be truly content.

Trying to please yourself or your friends or the world will never bring lasting happiness and satisfaction. That only comes by fulfilling the role God planned for you when He gave you new birth by His Holy Spirit. Unless you strive and work to please the Lord, you will never please yourself or anyone else. And unless you please God, you cannot expect to benefit from the ministry of His holy angels.

We Christians must come into unity. We must set aside our differences of doctrine and come into what Paul calls **the unity of the faith** (Eph. 4:13). It pleases God to see His children love one another and worship Him together in unity and harmony. But even that is not enough. We must also fulfill the plan He has laid out for us individually. As each of us finds his own unique place in the Kingdom, then and only then will God's Master Plan finally work out smoothly and effectively. Only then can you and I expect the ministering spirits to truly be able to work *all* things together for our good.

4

Be Obedient

How do you please God? You please Him by being obedient to Him. The Old Testament prophet Samuel said, **Hath the Lord as great delight in burnt offerings and sacrifices, as in obeying the voice of the Lord? Behold, to obey is better than sacrifice, and to hearken than the fat of rams** (1 Sam. 15:22).

But how do we obey God? By doing what He tells us to do — whether we want to or not, whether we like it or not, whether it makes sense to us or not. Let me give you an example.

When I am conducting a meeting, if the Lord directs me to have the same song sung again and again, I do it. Even though sometimes it may seem to be taking too much time. I can't help how much time it takes. If God says to do it, then I must obey. The greatest respect you can show the Lord is to do what He tells you to do. Jesus said to His disciples, **And why call ye me, Lord, Lord, and do not the things which I say?** (Luke 6:46). If we are to please God, we must do the things which He says.

One time I was speaking in a convention, and Brother Kenneth Copeland was leading the song service. At the Lord's direction I kept telling Brother Ken to keep on singing the same song over and over. Finally, he turned to the congregation and said, "Well, you know when Brother Norvel says to sing it, you may as well sing it!" He did it, and the Holy Spirit came into that meeting and ministered to the people in a mighty way. When God is leading, don't try to change directions. Be obedient.

I have heard people say, "Yes, but we were getting tired of that same song."

My answer is, "Who cares if you're tired? The Holy Ghost doesn't get tired. If God approves of that song and says to use it, *do it!*"

Obedience is better than sacrifice. Because obedience *is* sacrifice; it is sacrificing your desire in order to see God's desire fulfilled. If you will do that, you will be blessed. God will send His angels to minister to you and for you.

Do It God's Way

About fifteen years ago John Osteen was one of America's most well-known evangelists. He was receiving invitations to speak from all over the country. Thousands of people attended his meetings. In those days, I thought John was the best preacher I had ever heard in my life.

Then one day while he was on an evangelistic trip overseas, the Lord spoke to him and told him, "I want you to go back home and become pastor of that little church in Houston, Texas."

"But, Lord," John protested, "I'm a worldwide evangelist. Surely You wouldn't ask me to give up a successful international ministry to go back and serve as pastor to 150 to 200 people in a converted feed barn!"

The reason John knew what that little church was like was because he was the one who had founded it. But he had left that little handful of people in that tin barn to go off and become a worldwide evangelist. So naturally he wasn't too wild about giving up his fame and success to go bury himself in some "hole in the wall" like that little struggling church.

"Surely You don't really mean for me to give up all this and go back to *that!*" he told the Lord.

"Yes, I do."

So John humbled himself and came back to the States. He went to the little church in Houston, Texas. He walked in to those 150 people and told them, "The Lord wants me to become pastor of this church." But the surprising thing was, they didn't want him!

"Oh, no," they told him. "We don't think the Lord has called you to lead this church. We already have a pastor."

Now that was a shock to John. He had thought they would welcome him back with open arms. After all, he was the one who had started that church. Here the Lord had called him back from a tremendously successful evangelistic ministry around the world in which he spoke to thousands of people each night to serve as pastor of a tin barn church with 150 people. And to top it all off, they didn't even want him! But despite their resistance and his own feelings, John insisted, "Yes, the Lord wants me to come back and be pastor of this church."

He kept telling them that until they finally agreed that maybe God had called him back after all. So he became pastor, thinking that since he was so well-known and respected around the country, it wouldn't be long before he was having crowds of hundreds of people. But it didn't happen that way. Hardly anybody new ever came. He put on all kinds of crusades, held weekly meetings; he organized week-long campmeetings; he did everything he could think of to attract people. Sometimes he invited four or five hundred people to a convention in his church, advertised the meeting nationwide and offered free meals to all those in attendance. But still nothing happened. The people just wouldn't come.

I was in that little church one Sunday night, and John asked me to speak at the regular Sunday evening service. There were less than three hundred people present, and John had been back in that church for four years! It was just unbelievable.

Finally one day the Lord spoke to John and asked him, "Are you convinced now that people are not interested in following you? Are you fully persuaded that you aren't anything without Me?" And John was quick to agree with the Lord!

Keep Your Eyes on the Lord

Now I can tell you how to build a church. You do it the same way John Osteen did — by looking to God and not to your own ability or the world's devices. Some people think the first thing you do to build a ministry is to get a mailing list. Wrong! You don't need a lot of names, you just need one name — **the name which is above every name** (Phil. 2:9). You need to get in contact with the Lord and let Him build His own church.

That's what John learned. God told him to take his mailing list and burn it. He directed him to quit looking for new people and instead to begin teaching the ones who were there how to worship Him in spirit and in truth.

The Lord reminded John of Acts 2:46,47:

And they, continuing daily with one accord in the temple, and breaking bread from house to house, did eat their meat with gladness and singleness of heart,

Praising God, and having favour with all the people. And the Lord added to the church daily such as should be saved.

"Quit running around all the time and working so hard to build this ministry," the Lord instructed him. "You just be obedient to Me, and *I'll* do the building."

Then the Lord had John assign two ministers to assist him in the ministry of helps. "I want you to stay home some of the days during the week to pray and seek My face," He told him, "so when you get up on Sunday morning you will have something to say. If the Holy Ghost wants to prophesy, let Him do so. There is much that the Holy Spirit wants to do in your midst, but it will not happen unless you pray.

"Always remember: you are the pastor, but I am the Great Shepherd. I run this church, not you. You just take orders from Me. You be obedient, and see what happens."

Watch God Work!

So that's exactly what John did. It wasn't long before the church was full, so they had to build a new building. The attendance was up to about nine hundred in each service. So about a year later, they had to build another, larger building. Then another, and another. Soon attendance was up to two thousand five hundred, and growing. Each time attendance increased, that church had to build a bigger building. And each time they built, the building was paid in full.

By 1980 that church had an auditorium which seated four thousand people. Brother Hagin, Brother Copeland and I were invited down to hold a meeting in that new facility, and we had to turn away about a thousand people the first night. We stayed there for four or five days. Later, after the convention, John called me at home. The Sunday morning after the meetings had closed, attendance was still four thousand! The church was full. Just two weeks before, the attendance was only two thousand five hundred. So immediately John began planning a new auditorium to seat ten thousand!

That church invites foreign missionaries to come and stay from two weeks to a month before they leave for the mission field. In one recent year, more than 180 missionaries took advantage of that offer. The church grounds were so saturated with the presence of the Lord, it came to be known as the "Oasis of Love."

Several years ago that one church gave $670,000 to missions. Do you realize that's more than $10,000 a week! Can you imagine one church writing a check every week for more than $10,000 and giving it to missions? Do you know that is more than some denominations give all year, denominations with three or four thousand churches.

What caused that to happen? Obedience. John and his people were obedient to the Lord, and He brought that to pass.

Why doesn't that kind of thing happen in every church? Because not every church is totally obedient to God.

What Will God Honor?

You must understand one thing: *We please God when we obey Him.* You can't please God by being a rebel against the Holy Ghost.

No church can have a form of religion and deny the power of the Gospel, yet still enjoy the blessings and approval of the Lord.

To deny the power of the Gospel is to prohibit the manifestation of the Holy Spirit and the ministry of angels.

Not all churches give the Lord a free rein to do as He wills in their midst. For example, some churches preach the message of salvation, so God honors that message and people get saved.

But some of those same churches will make fun of the baptism of the Holy Spirit and ridicule healing services. When they do, *God will not honor that kind of thinking.* So consequently very few (if any) Holy Spirit baptisms or genuine healings ever take place in those churches.

"But does God approve of their ministry?" you might ask.

Yes, to a certain degree. God honors faith and obedience as far as it goes. He approves of their ministry as far as He can, but when they get to the point where they begin to deny or reject any part of His overall ministry, that's where the Lord draws the line. He cannot and He will not promote or reward doubt and unbelief.

Such churches usually operate in some form of worship service devised by man, something they have dreamed up for themselves. God honors their worship as much as He is able, but like His Son, He cannot do many great works in their midst **because of their unbelief** (Mark 6:6). That's why so few mighty works are seen in most denominational church services.

In order for God to confirm the Word with signs following, the Word must first be preached, then believed and acted upon in faith. And that just doesn't happen in churches which deny the full gospel message. In essence God says to them, **According to your faith, be it unto you** (Matt. 9:29). That's why it is vitally important to obey the Lord by allowing the Holy Spirit to **come in the *fulness* of the blessing of the gospel of Christ.** (Rom. 15:29). Because people only receive what they have been taught to believe for.

Don't Tie God's Hands

Several years ago a minister from a certain fundamentalist denomination, the pastor of the church I had attended when I was a boy, came to me for prayer. Now this man was never my pastor — he had come to the church after I was grown. But both my mother and my brother had died of disease while members of that church. When this man

29

became pastor, he heard about me and came to me for consultation. He told me that he wanted to stay on as pastor of that church, but that he wasn't sure he would be able to because he wanted to teach those people that Jesus was not only the Savior, but also the Healer and the Baptizer in the Holy Spirit.

He asked me to go with him to the church. There we walked around the building, praying as we went that the Lord would be allowed to have His *full* will done in it. The pastor knew how my own family members, godly people, had been taken by disease while the church had prayed for "God's will" to be done. He knew it had been God's will for them to be saved physically, just as it was His will that they be saved spiritually. But he also knew that God could only work in accordance with the faith of His people.

"Brother Norvel," he told me, "I want to stay here and point out the truth to these dear people. They don't understand that Jesus wants to heal their bodies just as much as He wants to save their souls. They don't understand that He wants them to be filled with His Holy Spirit so they, too, can minister healing — physical, mental, emotional financial, and spiritual — to others."

"I know, Pastor," I said to him, "I know exactly what you're talking about. I was raised in this church, and I love it. But I also know what these people believe. I used to believe the same way myself. But once I got out and began to seek God on my own and started seeing Him do so many things I had been taught were not His will to do, it gave me a whole new outlook. That's exactly what these people need. But they will only see manifested what they believe. And it's hard for people to believe when they're either not taught the fullness of the Gospel or else taught *not* to believe."

That's the sad part. So many times pastors and church leaders teach their people *not* to believe in the fullness of the Gospel. And when they do that, they tie God's hands. Because the Lord can only do for people what they *believe* He will do. And they cannot believe what they have not *heard*. (Rom. 10:14.)

Hear the Word of the Lord

I remember when my daughter developed those forty-two ugly growths all over her body. God pulled me out of my body, swept me up into His holy presence and said to me, "Son, if you will curse the roots of those things in My name, they will die and fall off her."

Now notice carefully. I had never *heard* that message taught by any preacher — denominational or otherwise. But I heard the Lord tell me that — and I *believed* Him! That is faith. I believed God. But then because I believed what I had heard, I put it into action. I *did* what the Lord said to do. And that is *obedience.*

I did what the Lord told me to do and I did it the way He told me to do it. And it pleased Him. As a result, today my daughter is totally healed. But that would not have happened if I had not *heard,* or if I had not *believed,* or if I had not *acted.*

When you get to the place where you are so determined to receive from God that you will *seek* Him with all your heart, *hear* what He as to say to you personally, *believe* what He tells you, and then *act* on what His Word says — that's when you will please God. And pleasing God is the key to seeing angels minister on your behalf. That's what the writer of Hebrews meant when he said that without faith (seeking, hearing, believing, acting) it is impossible to please God; because whoever comes to Him must believe that He is, and that He rewards those who seek Him with all their heart. (Heb. 11:6.) That reward is seeing your angels go into action!

If You Love Me, Obey Me

No church will ever see the full manifestation of the Lord without being obedient enough to give Him full rein to do as He wills. The Lord always wills to do so much more than we are willing to allow Him to do. That's why most churches fall so far short of what God really has in mind for them to be.

"Yes, but many of those same churches you say are unsuccessful have hundreds, even thousands, of members. They have beautiful buildings and huge budgets. They do all kinds of good works in the community. They send out missionaries around the world. I don't see how you can possibly say they're not experiencing the fullness of the manifestation of God's Spirit."

I say that because there is a difference between having a dynamic ministry to people and seeing God work miracles, signs and wonders in your midst! How many genuine miracles are produced in that church auditorium? How many of those people in that church are being won to the Lord, being filled with His Spirit, being healed in their bodies, and how many of these people are worshipping and praising God because His presence is manifested in every service? When that begins to happen, then you can know that God is free to do as *He wills* in their midst.

Numbers are not the most important thing. No church should ever be judged just by the number of people on its role or in attendance at its services. I would rather be somewhere in a mission with fifteen people and see God at work, than to be in a meeting of fifteen thousand without the power and presence of the Lord. I know of a little church down in Crystal River, Florida, a tiny mission that seats only about 75 people. But the presence of the Lord is so manifested in that place, there have been times I thought the Lord was literally going to carry me off!

When Christians begin to experience the full presence and power of God in their churches, they will begin to turn the world upside down for the Lord! God will bless them mightily! But as long as people only look at numbers, as long as they are afraid or unwilling to turn their church over totally to the Lord to do with as He wills, it will never happen.

"Oh, but Brother Norvel, you shouldn't be so hard on those churches. After all, those people love the Lord just as much as you do."

I know they do. I'm not condemning anyone. I just happen to know that there is a difference between loving the Lord and obeying the Holy Spirit. It is possible to love the Lord and still not be obedient to the leadership of the Holy Ghost. And unless the Holy Spirit is in *full* control, God is not pleased.

5

Follow the Holy Spirit's Leading

The greatest deliverance you will ever receive is deliverance from yourself.

Now what do I mean by that statement? I'm talking about getting into God's will. It is wonderful to be born again and set free from bondage to sin and Satan. But after that, you must keep yourself delivered. And many times the thing you need deliverance from most is your own self. That is, the power of your own mind.

You see, Satan is a liar and a deceiver. He knows that we want to follow the leadership of God's Holy Spirit, so he speaks to us in our minds just as the Holy Spirit does. When God tells us something, the devil speaks up inside to "warn" us not to listen. That's why it is so important to be able to distinguish between the voice of the Lord and the voice of the liar!

Move When the Waters Are Troubled

One evening when Charles Capps spoke in our church, I knew the Holy Ghost wanted me to minister in tongues, interpretation and prophecy before I introduced Charles. But I didn't want to do that. Why? Because when you have a quality man like Charles Capps who is the head of as large and valuable a ministry as his, naturally you don't want to do anything to cause him a delay. You just want to say a few words of introduction and then turn the service over to him to minister as he feels led of the Lord.

Unless the waters are troubled, that is. Now what do I mean? I mean that down in my spirit I could sense that the Holy Spirit wanted me to do something. I've been working for the Lord a long time now, and I know His voice when I hear it. I also know that I need to obey that voice. Ultimately I'm not responsible to a church or a denomination or even to a guest speaker. I am responsible to the Lord to do as He tells me to do.

So although it was hard for me to delay Brother Charles, I did as the Lord instructed. I spoke in tongues and the interpretation came. The Spirit ministered to several people in the meeting. The angels of the Lord ministered to the people as I gave them leave to do so by being obedient to the leading of the Spirit of God. As a result, I was blessed along with those people because of my obedience. I believe Brother Charles also was blessed.

Let the Spirit Lead

There is a difference between obeying God by ministering as the Holy Spirit gives you direction and just doing something because you want to do it. *The difference is the anointing.* Many times when people speak in tongues and give the interpretation, they are actually operating under a familiar spirit which makes them feel "religious." They are *not under direct orders from God Himself.* When you are operating in the power of the Holy Spirit, you don't have to tell people it's God at work — they will know it, and so will you!

How will they know? How will you know? By the *anointing* which is present. Remember: It is the anointing that breaks the yoke! (Is. 10:27.) You would be amazed at the number of churches which operate without the anointing. They plan their services and go through a form of what they call worship. They sing about two or three

36

hymns, say a prayer or two, take up an offering, and then finish up with a ten-minute message. That's it.

"What good can possibly come of that?" you ask.

There is always some good when the Word of God is preached, even in a cut-and-dried service like that. God's Word is so powerful that if any pastor just quotes a verse or two of it from his pulpit, the Holy Spirit will bless those who hear it. I would never say that no good ever comes out of reading the Bible or preaching from the Word of God.

In fact, it would be profitable to just read the Bible to a congregation without comment. I really believe that if you could get up in front of a congregation and do nothing but read five selected chapters from the Bible and then wait five minutes to allow the Holy Spirit to deal with people's hearts, there would be some who would get saved. And it doesn't matter what the denomination of the church might be. **God is no respecter of persons.** (Acts 10:34.) Wherever His Word is sown, His Holy Spirit is there to bring forth a harvest. If pastors will just *talk about Jesus,* there will always be some good to come of their message.

But there is a more effective way to minister. It is one thing to try to operate a church service by a humanly devised plan; but it is another thing to allow the Holy Spirit to do as He wills, to set free the angels of God to minister to the needs of people.

I remember the time I spoke in a denominational church in Atlanta, Georgia. We had a tremendous meeting. Many, many people were ministered to and blessed. After the conference was over, the pastor of that church came to me and said, "You know, I've been here seven years, and I've never seen the power of God as strong in this place as it has been while you were here."

This was a big beautiful church that would hold about a thousand people. During the time I held meetings in that church, we had to bring in extra chairs every night. The pastor couldn't believe what he was seeing take place in his own church.

"Brother Norvel," he said to me, "any time you want to come and hold a seminar here for three days or a week, or even a month, you're welcome. My pulpit is always open to you, you can do anything you want to do. I'll step out of my pulpit every Sunday and turn it over to you if you'll come and speak to us." And that was the first time I had ever been in his church! Why did this happen? Because I allowed the Spirit of God to lead.

Witness to Others

Just before His ascension into heaven, Jesus told His disciples, **But ye shall receive power, after that the Holy Ghost is come upon you: and ye shall be witnesses unto me both in Jerusalem, and in all Judaea, and in Samaria, and unto the uttermost part of the earth** (Acts 1:8). Angels work with people who follow the leading of the Holy Spirit. And one of the greatest things the Holy Spirit does is to lead believers to witness to others about Jesus Christ.

"You mean soul-winning is part of the ministry of helps?"

It sure is; in fact, it's the Number One ministry of helps. By leading a person to the Lord you are helping him to find eternal life hereafter and abundant life here and now. What could be a bigger help to anyone than that?

"Yes, that may be so. But, Brother Norvel, that's just not my ministry. I'm not called to witness."

Oh, yes you are. I know you are . . . you just don't know it.

You see, as Christians it is always our ministry to talk to others about Jesus, to lead people to a saving knowledge of the Lord. With the presence and power of the Holy Spirit within, it should be the most natural thing in the world for a believer to want to share his faith with those he comes in contact with every day. Yet so many Christians seem to think they can't do it.

"But I don't have any *experience* in that sort of thing," they say.

All right then. Let me tell you how to get some experience. You start out by just passing out tracts. You don't have to say a word, just let the printed page do your talking for you. Then you can move up to inviting people to church services. That way, you still don't have to present the plan of salvation; all you have to do is bring someone to church with you where he can hear the Gospel preached.

You see, witnessing doesn't necessarily mean sitting down with a sinner, opening your Bible and trying to win him to the Lord yourself. If you honestly feel you can't do that effectively, then just bring the sinner to someone who can do that. Compel people to come. How? By showing them the love of Jesus. If you show people the love of Christ, they will want to know what you have that they don't. People respond to love. Go out and sincerely love people, and you'll find that sooner or later they will become interested in what you have. You'll also find it's not that hard to tell them when they really want to know.

Some time ago I was in Tulsa, Oklahoma, for a meeting. While I was there a college student, a fraternity boy, offered to carry my luggage for me. He wasn't a bell boy, he was a Spirit-filled, full-time worker for the Lord. He had been wanting to talk to me for a long time, so he found his chance by offering to carry my bags.

"Boy, that campus ministry you have, Brother Norvel," he told me, "that's something else. I was on campus one day, and one of your people started talking to me about Jesus. I had just stopped to buy some stationery from him, and he began to show me all these tracts about Jesus. That guy was really a good witness for the Lord. 'Course I was already saved, but I was really impressed by this guy's approach to witnessing."

Then he shook his head in appreciation. "I gotta hand it to you, Brother Norvel, you really know how to reach folks for the Lord. I watched your people all afternoon. They would sell stationery and then start talking about Jesus. That's really a good way to get the job done."

"Thank you," I replied. "You're right. It works great."

I wish I could take credit for that idea, but it wasn't mine. The Lord showed me years ago that He wanted me to do that. He gave me the plan of sending teams of young people to college campuses all over the country. They go in disguised as stationery salesmen. Although they make a little money that way, it's not really their purpose. Their main objective is to witness to students about the Lord.

That is the way it should be for every Christian. Although we "make a living" by teaching, or running a business, or working in a factory, our real purpose in life should be to share Jesus with everyone we meet. As Christians we are to put the Lord first in everything we do. That's what I do. My businesses are just a sideline with me. My real purpose and goal in life is not to make money or even earn a living — it's to share Jesus with as many people as I possibly can.

Now that doesn't mean that we are to try to shove Jesus down everybody's throat. It just means that we should make Jesus our "business," and in a relaxed and natural way share

His love with others. It will take wisdom to do that. You'll have to pray for it. But God will give it to you.

Anyone who will mix the wisdom and love of Christ in his business in order to share the Gospel with the world had better look out. God will bless him so much he won't know where it's all coming from. The Lord has been doing that to me for years. He blesses me so much I can hardly stand it!

Why, He even blesses those who work with me. If a person goes to work for me, he'd better get ready to be blessed. Now he'll have to stay sweet and walk in love. No one can go around talking against me or this ministry God has given me, and still expect God's blessings to fall on him.

Guard Your Mouth

The angels of God won't minister to you if you talk against God's ministers. They will stand off in the distance and look sad because you are so stupid not to know any better than to judge and criticize God's servants. If you are guilty of that, you need to realize that your worst enemy is your own mouth. God desires to bless you all the time, but when your mouth is out of line with His Word, He can't.

Don't make the mistake of judging and finding fault with other ministries and ministers. For one thing, you don't have any right to do that. As Paul said, **Who art thou that judgest another man's servant? to his own master he standeth or falleth. Yea, he shall be holden up: for God is able to make him stand** (Rom. 14:4). The only person you are free to judge is yourself. (2 Cor. 13:5.)

If you don't agree with what is being done in some ministry, then start your own. Then you can make all the decisions — and all the mistakes! You can talk all you want to about your own ministry. But when it comes to other ministries and ministers, you would do well to watch your mouth!

Why? Because judging and condemning other Christians, especially those who are about their Father's business, is not pleasing to the Lord. And unless a person is pleasing God, his angels won't work for him.

To be blessed, you've got to be a blessing. And if you want to be a blessing, then follow the leading of the Holy Spirit. He'll show you what to do!

6

Rely on the Word of God

Jesus said unto him, Thou shalt love the Lord thy God with all thy heart, and with all thy soul, and with all thy mind.

This is the first and great commandment.

And the second is like unto it, Thou shalt love thy neighbour as thyself.

On these two commandments hang all the law and the prophets.

Matthew 22:37-40

Here Jesus gives us the "formula" for keeping our angels on the job. We must fulfill these two requirements: We must love the Lord our God, and we must also love our neighbor as ourselves. Otherwise, our angels cannot minister to us or for us.

"But I've never even *seen* an angel," some people tell me. "So how can I really believe they are busy ministering on my behalf?"

The answer to that question is simple. You believe it because the Bible says it. You accept the Bible by faith. Faith — believing God — is the first prerequisite to pleasing Him. But you have to do that yourself. It doesn't matter how talented you are, or how intelligent, or how beautiful, or what a good life you live. All that is wonderful, but none of it has anything to do with faith. Faith is believing God. And that you must do on your own. No one else can do it for you.

But do you know that the Church of Jesus Christ as a whole doesn't know much about that? That's why about half of the Church is sick, and the other half has financial needs, and neither half knows what to do about it.

Yet the answer is so simple. *You read the Word of God, believe it, and do what it says.*

Take the matter of financial needs for example. What is the answer to that? Jesus gave it to us in Matthew 6:33, **But seek ye first the kingdom of God, and his righteousness; and all these things shall be added unto you.**

In that same passage from the Sermon on the Mount, the Lord told us not to worry about food or clothing or any of these other things the world spends its time and energy seeking after. He said that if we would just put God and His righteousness *first* in our lives, then we wouldn't have any needs to worry about because they would be filled for us. By whom? By the ministering angels. That's what they're there for, **to minister for them who shall be the heirs of salvation** (Heb. 1:14).

"Yes, but you don't realize I've got *needs*!"

I know that. So does God. And He also has a plan for meeting those needs. *Your biggest need is to find out God's plan!* That plan is the answer to all your other needs! And it's simple. You find it in the Bible: "Put God *first* in your life, and these other things you need will be added unto you."

"But how will God add them to me?"

I don't know. That's His problem. Don't worry about time or conditions or any of those things; that's as bad as worrying about the needs themselves. You just work and strive to please God, and He will see to the rest. And one way you please God is to believe His Word.

Stand on the Word

Then was Jesus led up of the Spirit into the wilderness to be tempted of the devil.

And when he had fasted forty days and forty nights, he was afterward an hungred.

And when the tempter came to him, he said, If thou be the Son of God, command that these stones be made bread.

But he answered and said, It is written, Man shall not live by bread alone, but by every word that proceedeth out of the mouth of God.

Matthew 4:1-4

The devil is a liar. Jesus called him the father of liars. (John 8:44.) His main weapon is deception; he tries to inject doubt into the believer. Notice what he said to Jesus here in this passage: *"If thou be the Son of God...."* Now the devil knew who Jesus was because he had been in heaven with Him. Satan also knew what he had come to earth to accomplish. He knew that Jesus came to take on Himself the sins of the world that we might be set free. He knew that the stripes Jesus would bear on His back would be payment in full for our healing. That's why he tried to trick Jesus into giving up His mission before it ever began. He tried his best to get Jesus to doubt His identity and purpose.

But Jesus was too wise to fall into Satan's trap. Jesus knew who He was. He knew it by the testimony of the Holy Spirit who lived inside Him. He also knew that His Father expected Him to be obedient and to live by faith, just as we are expected to be obedient and live by faith — faith in the Word of God. Jesus took His stand on the integrity of God's Word, and that's what we must do if we are to please our heavenly Father: **Now the just shall live by faith: but if any man draw back, my soul shall have no pleasure in him** (Heb. 10:38).

45

To live by faith means that we must do as Jesus did and resist temptation. To resist temptation means to obey God and disobey the devil.

Satan will bring all kinds of temptation to us. Most of the time that temptation will come first as a thought — just as this temptation to doubt His relationship to God came to Jesus. But Jesus resisted that temptation. He refused to submit to carnal thoughts. Instead, He chose to take His stand on the Word of God. That's what you must do if you want to be pleasing to God as Jesus was.

Apply the Word

Then the devil taketh him up into the holy city, and setteth him on a pinnacle of the temple,

And saith unto him, If thou be the Son of God, cast thyself down: for it is written, He shall give his angels charge concerning thee: and in their hands they shall bear thee up, lest at any time thou dash thy foot against a stone.

Jesus said unto him, It is written again, Thou shalt not tempt the Lord thy God.

Matthew 4:5-7

Notice that Satan didn't give up after one temptation. Here he comes again with the same approach. **If thou be the Son of God, cast thyself down....** The devil *knew* who Jesus was, yet he still tried to cause Him to doubt, to *prove* who He was by putting God to the test. If the devil would do that with Jesus Himself, you can be sure he'll try it with you and me — not just once, but over and over.

But notice also how Jesus relied on the Word of God. He applied that Word to the devil. Satan even tried to quote scripture to Jesus to convince Him that it was all right for Him to put God to the test. But notice that Jesus was not fooled; He knew that scriptures can be twisted by the enemy to say things God never intended. *Jesus not only knew the Word, He knew how to apply the Word!*

46

Now let's see how that relates to our lives. Many times when people hear the good news that the stripes that Jesus bore on His back paid the price for their healing, they have trouble accepting it. Even though it is recorded at least three times in the scriptures. (Is. 53:5; Matt. 8:17; 1 Pet. 2:24.) Either they have been taught *not* to believe it refers to physical healing, or else they don't know how to apply it to their own personal lives. Therefore, although it is true, the Word doesn't "work" for them because they don't apply that Word by faith.

Scriptures applied in faith work *all* the time. But the Word has to be applied from *personal* knowledge. It won't work just because you heard someone else say it in some gospel service six months ago. *Working* faith causes God to manifest Himself. And working faith is faith which is accompanied by corresponding action. James tells us that faith without works (action) is dead. (James 2:17.) So it's not enough to *believe* the Word, you then must *apply* what you believe. You do that by *acting* on the Word.

You can memorize the entire New Testament and believe it with all your heart, but if you don't put action to your faith, it's dead. That's why Paul said that the letter of the law **killeth, but the spirit giveth life.** (2 Cor. 3:6.)

The "spirit" of the law is the Holy Spirit of God. So you see, the Holy Spirit and the Word agree. They are in total harmony. Unless you remember that fact and keep yourself in line with it, you'll be robbed of your blessing. You have to have respect for the Holy Spirit. You have to expect Him to do what the Word says He will do. God's Holy Spirit is not pleased when He is not allowed to express Himself the way He wants to for those in need and in trouble.

So if you want to please God, you have to apply His Word. If you are like those people who have a hard time accepting that the stripes of Jesus paid for physical healing, you need to do just what Jesus did in these scriptures: **Jesus said unto him, It is written....** You need to start *saying* the scriptures.

Look up those verses that declare that you were healed by the stripes of Jesus. Memorize them. Learn them by heart. Then every time Satan comes against you to suggest that you're not healed, every time you feel pain or symptoms of that sickness or disease, resist the enemy by quoting the Word as Jesus did. Say to the devil: "It is written, by the stripes of Jesus I am healed. Jesus is my Savior and my Healer. His healing power is at work in me right now restoring my health."

Do that continuously all day, every day. Remind yourself that you do not live by sight (or feelings), but by every word that proceeds out of the mouth of God.

If you will take your stand on God's Word, believing it in your heart and applying it by your mouth, then sooner or later you will see your healing manifested:

> **But what saith it? The word is nigh thee, even in thy mouth, and in thy heart: that is, the word of faith, which we preach;**
>
> **That if thou shalt confess with thy mouth..., and shalt believe in thine heart..., thou shalt be saved (healed, made whole).**
>
> **Romans 10:8,9**

It pleases God for His children to believe His Word and act on it. If you will do that, He will send His angels to minister to you.

Don't Let Satan Pressure You

Did you notice in Matthew 4:6 that Satan tried to put Jesus under pressure? He quoted scripture to Him, insinuating that if Jesus really had faith He would cast Himself down from the pinnacle of the temple and trust

God's angels to protect Him. That's another one of the devil's favorite tricks. Jesus didn't fall for it, and neither should you and I.

Remember: *Pressure is always from the devil. The Holy Spirit is a gentleman; He always leads gently and sweetly.*

That should be a help to you in learning to recognize whether a leading is from Satan or from the Lord. If any situation puts you under driving pressure, then you can be sure it's not from God, because like a good shepherd, our heavenly Father *leads* His children, He doesn't *drive* them: **And when he putteth forth his own sheep, he** *goeth before* **them, and the sheep** *follow* **him: for** *they know his voice* (John 10:4). Get to know the voice of the Holy Spirit, then you can follow His leading rather than being driven by pressure from the enemy.

I've had good friends — born-again, Spirit-filled, tongues-speaking, demon-chasing believers — who lost their lives because they allowed the devil to pressure them into doing something they should have known better than to do. Notice that Jesus didn't fall for Satan's trick to pressure Him into casting Himself down from the temple and relying on the angels to save Him. Our Lord knew that His angels were there to keep Him from dashing His foot against a stone. But He was also wise enough to know better than to go around kicking rocks just to see if they would intervene! Never be foolish enough to purposely get yourself in a mess just to test your angel power! Remember: Angels move in response to faith — not foolishness!

Don't fall for Satan's lies. If you're believing for your healing, don't let the devil trick you by saying that if you really were healed you wouldn't still be hurting. That's the most ridiculous statement I've ever heard. Yet I hear Christians repeating it all the time: "Well, I thought I was healed last week, but then the pain came back, so I guess I wasn't; I guess I'm still sick."

What has pain got to do with disease? *Pain is a symptom; it is not a disease.* Learn to tell the difference between sickness and symptoms, because Satan can lay symptoms on you anytime he wants to (if you let him). But he cannot legally place sickness on you, because Jesus has already borne that sickness *for* you.

This is one of those times you need to turn your attention from the physical to the spiritual. Here's where you have to take your stand on the Word of God. You have to affirm that according to God's Word you *are* healed, regardless of what your body may try to tell you. You dominate the physical by the spiritual, you don't let the physical override the spiritual. If you do, you'll fall right into Satan's trap.

Stand on God's Word of promise. God is a Spirit. What He speaks forth from His mouth is truth. If you'll be persistent and stand on that truth, it will set you free! The devil will leave and take his pain with him. **Because greater is He that is in you, than he that is in the world.** (1 John 4:4). And He that is in you will give His angels charge over you to keep you in all your ways.

Don't Trust Feelings

Some people tell me, "Brother Norvel, I know now that I made a terrible mistake in the past, but at the time I just *felt* like it was the thing to do."

Never do anything because you *feel* like it is the thing to do. As Christians we are to be lead by the Holy Spirit, not by *feelings*. If you set out to follow feelings, the devil will see to it that you feel what he wants you to feel. Going by feelings can lead you into all kinds of trouble, because feelings can lie to you. But the Holy Ghost won't lie to you. The Bible doesn't lie.

If you are making a decison right now about marriage, investing money, changing jobs, moving your family or some other important event in your life, don't go by what you feel. Ask the Holy Spirit to guide you. Wait upon the Lord. Be patient. Sometimes the Holy Spirit needs time to work things out for you. God works miracles, signs and wonders for His children. But He doesn't always do them overnight. God is not pressured. He takes His time and does things right. God doesn't get nervous about time, because He's got lots of it.

If you feel yourself getting under pressure, then you will know who it is who's putting it on you. It's the devil — every time. In God, there is no pressure.

When the Holy Spirit leads, there is peace and contentment. Whenever the enemy tries to get me all upset and confused I order him to shut up and get out! I don't let anything rob me of the peace of God and the joy of the Lord. I know they are more valuable to me than all the gold in this earth, because the joy of the Lord is my strength.

Be Strong and of Good Courage

Be strong and of a good courage: for unto this people shalt thou divide for an inheritance the land, which I sware unto their fathers to give them.

Only be thou strong and very courageous, that thou mayest observe to do according to all the law, . . . that thou mayest prosper whithersoever thou goest.

This book of the law shall not depart out of thy mouth; but thou shalt meditate therein day and night . . . : for then thou shalt make thy way prosperous, and then thou shalt have good success.

Joshua 1:6-8

. . .**Neither be ye sorry; for the joy of the Lord is your strength.**

Nehemiah 8:10

If you want to prosper and do well, if you want the angels of God to minister to you and for you, then heed these words. Stay in the Word of God. Meditate in it day and night. Let the peace and the joy of the Lord be your strength.

If you let the devil put pressure on you, I guarantee that you will lose that peace and joy. And if you're not careful, you'll make some foolish mistake or decision.

Once he has caused you to make a bad decision, the devil delights in jumping all over you about it. That's why he is called the accuser of the brethren. (Rev. 12:10.)

He'll pressure you into making a mistake, then accuse you for making it! He'll start suggesting that since you've gone this far, you may as well go all the way. And all the time the Holy Spirit will be telling you to stop, stop, stop!

That's when you need to listen to the still, small voice of the Lord. Get still and hear from the Father. Tell Him you've missed it, and you're sorry. Then the peace of the Lord will come flooding back in on you like a river. The joy of the Lord will be your strength. His angels will come and encamp round about you.

7

Worship the Lord

Again, the devil taketh him up into an exceeding high mountain, and sheweth him all the kingdoms of the world, and the glory of them;

And saith unto him, All these things will I give thee, if thou wilt fall down and worship me.

Then saith Jesus unto him, Get thee hence, Satan: for it is written, Thou shalt worship the Lord thy God, and him only shalt thou serve.

Matthew 4:8-10

One of the most important ways of pleasing God is by worshipping Him. That's why Satan tried to tempt Jesus into sinning against the Father by offering Him all the kingdoms of the earth if He would just bow down and worship him. He knew that what a person worships is the thing he becomes a servant to: **Thou shalt worship the Lord thy God, and him only shalt thou** *serve.*

In a sense, that's exactly what happened to Adam and Eve in the Garden of Eden. Satan convinced them that he knew more than God, so they listened to him rather than to their loving Father. As a result, they lost their earthly kingdom to the devil. They became slaves to sin instead of servants of righteousness.

That's what Satan tried to get Jesus to do. He tried to tempt Him into acknowledging him as king of the earth rather than God. But Jesus was far too wise to fall for Satan's trick.

53

Are you? Did you know that when you sin, what you are actually doing is siding with Satan against God? Like Adam and Eve, you are taking the word of a fallen angel rather than standing on the Word of Almighty God, Maker of heaven and earth. To choose Satan is to serve Satan. In essence, when you give your body to sin you are falling down and worshipping the devil.

"Oh, no, I'd never do that!"

Well, if you wouldn't worship the devil, then why do you listen to him and do what he wants you to do instead of listening to God and doing what pleases Him? What is worship but obedience and service?

You see, there are two spiritual fathers in this world. Every day of your life you must make a choice of which one you will serve. Either you serve the Father of Light, or you serve the father of liars! The one you choose is the one you will serve. The choice is up to you.

Choose You This Day

I call heaven and earth to record this day against you, that I have set before you life and death, blessing and cursing: therefore choose life, that both thou and thy seed may live.
Deuteronomy 30:19

In this passage the Lord gave the children of Israel a choice of whom they would serve: Him or the enemy. That same choice is given to each of us. If you refuse Satan and choose to follow the Lord, you can enjoy abundant life on this earth, and eternal life in heaven hereafter. But if you choose to live in sin, you will reap the consequences of that lifestyle. The choice is up to you.

You would be surprised to know that some people actually *choose* to follow Satan. Some have told me, "I don't want to follow God. I don't want to go to heaven. I want to live my life the way I choose. If that leads to hell, that's my business. I'll just go be with my friends. At least there I can do what I please." I try to talk them out of that choice, but the final decision is theirs.

All these things will I give thee, if thou wilt fall down and worship me. Jesus had the same choice you and I have. But notice the choice He made. **Get thee hence, Satan: for it is written, Thou shalt worship the Lord thy God, and him only shalt thou serve** (v. 10).

That should be our response to Satan every time he comes to tempt or trick us into serving him instead of the Lord. If you want to be pleasing to God, then make up your mind right now that every day for the rest of your life you are going to serve the Lord your God.

Under what conditions? Under any and all conditions! If God calls you to be a missionary in Africa, then your reaction ought to be, "Praise God, I'm on my way to Africa. I'm going to live a life of peace and joy there if I have to live in a mud hut and ride a zebra to breakfast!"

On the other hand, if the Lord should choose to place you in a penthouse on Fifth Avenue in New York, just say: "Very well, I'll live in a penthouse in New York, wear tweed suits and a wool overcoat and find the joy of the Lord by winning New Yorkers to Jesus!"

Just Be Yourself

Wherever God sends you, wear the kind of clothes those people wear and eat the kind of foods they eat. When Jesus sent out the seventy to minister in His name, He commanded them: **And into whatsoever city ye enter, and they receive you, eat such things as are set before you** (Luke 10:8). In First Corinthians 9:19-22, Paul says that wherever he went he became as the people he lived among, that he might by all means save some. That's a good example to follow. If you're sent to a foreign country, learn to speak their language so you can communicate the glorious Gospel of Jesus Christ to them.

The town or the country you live in makes no difference. Your outer garments don't really matter. What you eat and drink is not the main thing: **For the kingdom of God is not meat and drink; but righteousness, and peace, and joy in the Holy Ghost** (Rom. 14:17). None of these exterior things have anything to do with serving the Lord. It's *joy* in the Holy Ghost that really matters!

Wherever you are, wherever He sends you, the Lord wants you to be you. It's good to learn from other people, just as you learn from the Bible. But you can learn from others without losing your own individual personality and identity. God made you exactly as you are. He wants you to be your own unique self. It's fine to admire and respect someone else. Just don't try to be someone else. Be yourself. Because *you* are pleasing to God!

Now not everyone may like you as you are. That's fine. They don't have to like you or agree with you. People sometimes tell me they don't like my looks or the way I preach or what I believe. That's okay. God loves me and accepts me, and He's the one I'm trying to please, not other people. That should be your attitude.

Learn to listen to God. Take on His nature. Learn of Him. Let Him train you for whatever He has in mind for you. Let Him mold you into His image and likeness. Do you know what happens when God starts changing you? It's so sweet. You walk from glory to glory!

It pleases God when you become like Him, because then you truly begin to love the Lord your God with all your heart and mind and strength. And you begin to love your neighbor as *yourself*. That's one of the greatest benefits of selling out totally to God: You learn to love *yourself*. The self God made you to be.

Then Shall He Send His Angels!

Then the devil leaveth him, and, behold, angels came and ministered unto him.

Matthew 4:11

Notice what happened to Jesus after He had resisted Satan's temptations. **Angels came and ministered unto him.** The word "angels" is plural. Angels came to minister to our Lord. And they will come and minister to you too! When? Right now.

If you will do those things which please God, He will send His holy angels to minister to you and for you and through you. They will help you and uplift you and bring you victory!

Glory to God forever!

Books by Norvel Hayes

How To Live and Not Die

The Winds of God
Bring Revival

God's Power Through
the Laying on of Hands

Know Your Enemy

The Blessing of Obedience

Stand in the Gap
for Your Children

How To Get
Your Prayers Answered

Holy Spirit Gifts Series

Number One Way
To Fight the Devil

Why You Should
Speak in Tongues

Prostitute Faith

You Must Confess
Your Faith

What To Do for Healing

God's Medicine of Faith —
The Word

How To Triumph
Over Sickness

Financial Dominion —
How To Take Charge
of Your Finances

The Healing Handbook

Rescuing Souls
From Hell —
Handbook for
Effective Soulwinning

How To Cast Out Devils

Power for Living

Radical Christianity

Secrets To Keeping
Your Faith Strong

Putting Your Angels
To Work

**Available from your local bookstore,
or by writing:**

Harrison House
P. O. Box 35035 • Tulsa, OK 74153

Norvel Hayes shares God's Word boldly and simply, with an enthusiasm that captures the heart of the hearer. He has learned through personal experience that God's Word can be effective in every area of life and that it will work for anyone who will believe it and apply it.

Norvel owns several businesses which function successfully despite the fact that he spends more than half his time away from the office, ministering the Gospel throughout the country. His obedience to God and his willingness to share his faith have taken him to a variety of places. He ministers in churches, seminars, conventions, colleges, prisons — anywhere the Spirit of God leads.

For a complete list of tapes and books
by Norvel Hayes, write:
Norvel Hayes
P. O. Box 1379
Cleveland, TN 37311
*Feel free to include your prayer requests and comments
when you write.*